IT'S TIME TO EAT GREEN PEPPER

It's Time to Eat GREEN PEPPER

Walter the Educator

Silent King Books
A WhichHead Entertainment Imprint

Copyright © 2025 by Walter the Educator

All rights reserved. No part of this book may be reproduced in any manner whatsoever without written per- mission except in the case of brief quotations embodied in critical articles and reviews.

First Printing, 2024

Disclaimer

This book is a literary work; the story is not about specific persons, locations, situations, and/or circumstances unless mentioned in a historical context. Any resemblance to real persons, locations, situations, and/or circumstances is coincidental. This book is for entertainment and informational purposes only. The author and publisher offer this information without warranties expressed or implied. No matter the grounds, neither the author nor the publisher will be accountable for any losses, injuries, or other damages caused by the reader's use of this book. The use of this book acknowledges an understanding and acceptance of this disclaimer.

It's Time to Eat GREEN PEPPER is a collectible early learning book by Walter the Educator suitable for all ages belonging to Walter the Educator's Time to Eat Book Series. Collect more books at WaltertheEducator.com

USE THE EXTRA SPACE TO TAKE NOTES AND DOCUMENT YOUR MEMORIES

GREEN PEPPER

It's time to eat, come take a peek,

It's Time to Eat
Green Pepper

A veggie crisp and fresh this week!

So big and green, so smooth and round,

A crunchy snack that's safe and sound!

Green peppers grow on plants so tall,

Hiding there until we call.

We pick them up and hold them tight,

Shiny, firm, and such a sight!

We wash them well and make them clean,

So bright and fresh, a perfect green!

Drip, drop, shake them dry,

Now they're ready, oh, my, my!

We slice them up, so crisp, so neat,

Little rings so fun to eat!

Some are big and some are small,

Crunchy circles, grab them all!

It's Time to Eat Green Pepper

Eat them raw or cook them hot,

In a salad or a pot!

Dip them, roast them, fry them too,

So many ways, what will you do?

Green peppers taste so fresh and sweet,

A little juicy, fun to eat!

Not too spicy, just just right,

A veggie full of pure delight!

They're good for you and help you grow,

They give you strength from head to toe!

Full of color, full of cheer,

A tasty treat all through the year!

On pizza, pasta, soups, or rice,

Green peppers make it all so nice!

Toss them in, give them a try,

It's Time to Eat
Green Pepper

A burst of flavor, oh, my, my!

So when you see that color shine,

Pick a pepper, it's just fine!

Take a bite, hear the crunch,

A perfect snack for any lunch!

Now we're full and feeling bright,

Green peppers make us feel just right!

Crispy, tasty, fresh, and new,

It's Time to Eat
Green Pepper

Try some peppers, they're good for you!

ABOUT THE CREATOR

Walter the Educator is one of the pseudonyms for Walter Anderson. Formally educated in Chemistry, Business, and Education, he is an educator, an author, a diverse entrepreneur, and he is the son of a disabled war veteran. "Walter the Educator" shares his time between educating and creating. He holds interests and owns several creative projects that entertain, enlighten, enhance, and educate, hoping to inspire and motivate you. Follow, find new works, and stay up to date with Walter the Educator™ at WaltertheEducator.com

www.ingramcontent.com/pod-product-compliance
Lightning Source LLC
LaVergne TN
LVHW052012060526
838201LV00059B/3996